PIANO / VOCAL / GUITAR

M000160125

Celtic Thunder
HERITAGE

ISBN 978-1-4584-0285-1

HAL•LEONARD® CORPORATION

7777 W. BLUEMOUND RD. P.O. BOX 13819 MILWAUKEE, WI 53213

Visit Hal Leonard Online at
www.halleonard.com

THE DUTCHMAN

Words and Music by
MICHAEL SMITH

Long a-go ____ I used to be ____ a young ____ man, ____ but dear Mar - g'ret re-mem- - bers that for me. ____

The

BUACHAILL O' EIRNE

Arranged by
PHIL COULTER

BLACK IS THE COLOUR

Arranged by
PHIL COULTER

MY LOVE IS LIKE A RED RED ROSE

Arranged by
PHIL COULTER

Gentle ballad

HOME FROM THE SEA

Words and Music by
PHIL COULTER

With a highland lilt

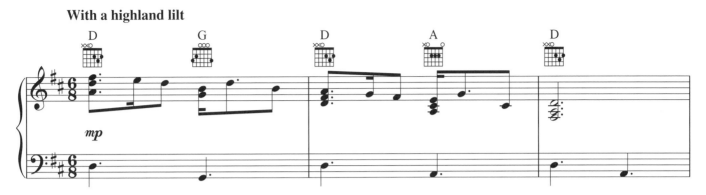

On a cold win-ter's night with a storm at its height, the
bat - tled their way past the mouth of the bay, it was
back in the town on a street that runs down to the

life - boat an - swered the call. They pitched and they tossed 'til they
blow - ing like nev - er be - fore. As they gal - lant - ly fought, ev - 'ry
sea and the har - bor wall. They'd gath - ered in pairs at the

JUST A SONG AT TWILIGHT

Arranged by
PHIL COULTER

GALWAY GIRL

Written by
STEVE EARLE

NOREEN

Words and Music by
PHIL COULTER

hard - er _____ each day.

KINDRED SPIRITS

By PHIL COULTER

Moderate Ballad

WHISKEY IN THE JAR

Arranged by
PHIL COULTER

RED ROSE CAFÉ

Words and Music by
PIERRE KARTNER

A PLACE IN THE CHOIR

Written by
BILL STAINES

Moderately, in 2

All God's crea-tures got a place in the choir. Some sing low and

some sing high-er; some sing out loud on a tel-e-phone wire;

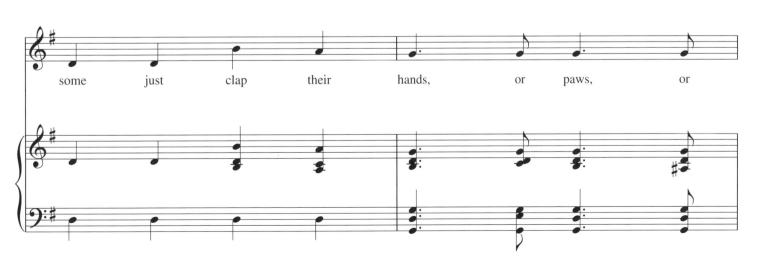

some just clap their hands, or paws, or

AMAZING GRACE

Arranged by
PHIL COULTER

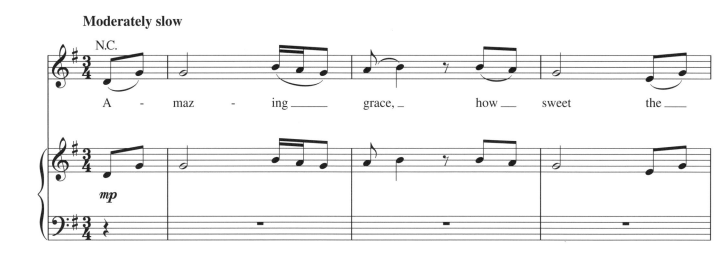

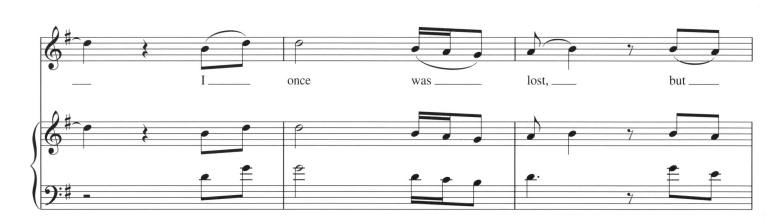

HOMES OF DONEGAL

Words and Music by
SEAN MACBRIDE

I'LL TELL ME MA/MUIRSHEEN DURKIN/COURTIN IN THE KITCHEN/ THE HOLY GROUND

Arranged by
PHIL COULTER

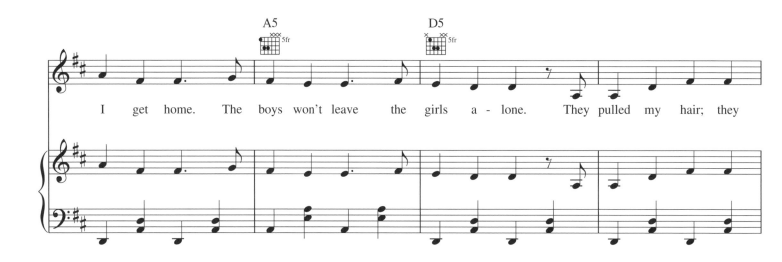

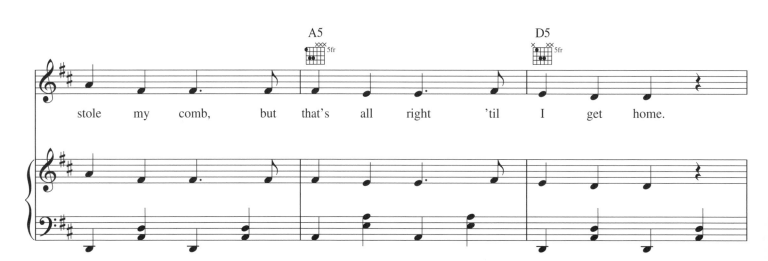

"Muirsheen Durkin"

"Courtin' in the Kitchen"

"The Holy Ground"

SKYE BOAT SONG

Arranged by
PHIL COULTER

TAKE ME HOME

Words and Music by
PHIL COULTER

WORKING MAN

Words and Music by
RITA MACNEIL

Moderately

Lyrics:

It's a work-ing man I am, ___ and I've
an-y length of time ___ I can

been down un-der-ground. ___ And I swear to God, ___ if I
hold it in my mind; ___ I

ev-er see the sun. Oh, for

dark re - cess ___ of the mine, where you age be - fore ___ your time ___

___ and the coal dust lies heav - y on your

lungs. It's a work-ing man I am, ___

___ and I've been down un - der - ground. ___ And I

You Raise Me Up

Words and Music by BRENDAN GRAHAM
and ROLF LOVLAND

*Recorded a half step higher.